I0813145

Desserts from Around the World

An Imprint of Pop!
popbooksonline.com

PASTRIES FROM AROUND THE WORLD

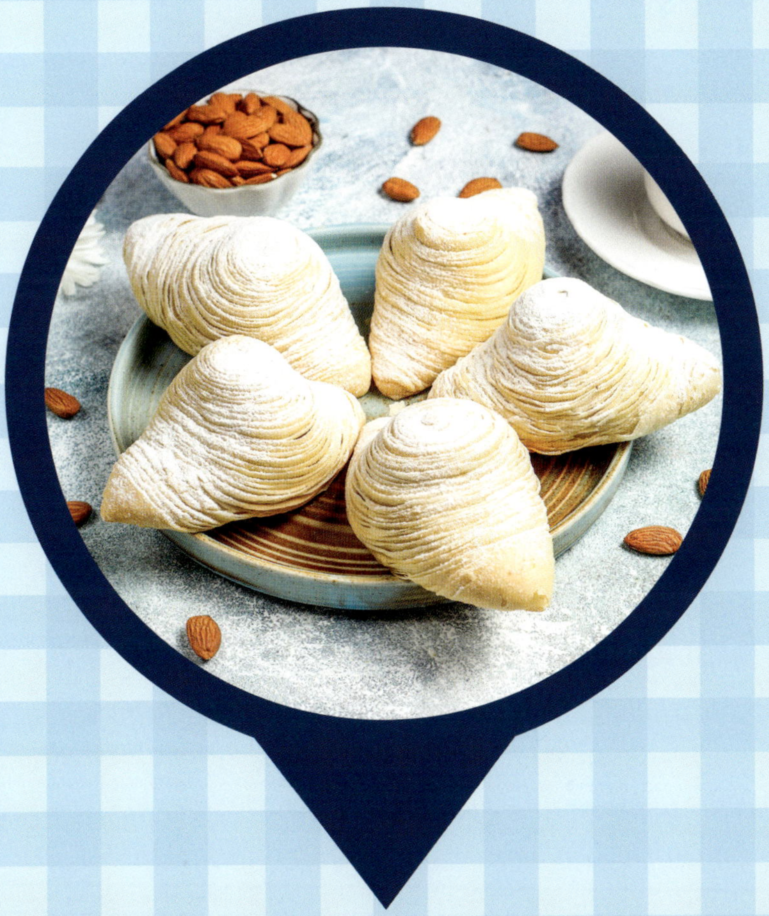

by Grace Hansen

WELCOME TO DiscoverRoo!

This book is filled with videos, puzzles, games, and more! Scan the QR codes* while you read, or visit the website below to make this book pop.

popbooksonline.com/pastry

abdobooks.com

Published by Pop!, a division of ABDO, PO Box 398166, Minneapolis, Minnesota 55439.

Printed in the United States of America, North Mankato, Minnesota.

102024
012025

Cover Photo: Getty Images
Interior Photos: Shutterstock Images, Getty Images
Editor: Elizabeth Andrews
Series Designer: Laura Graphenteen

Library of Congress Control Number: 2024938614

Publisher's Cataloging-in-Publication Data

Names: Hansen, Grace, author.
Title: Pastries from around the world / by Grace Hansen
Description: Minneapolis, Minnesota : Pop!, 2025 | Series: Desserts from around the world | Includes online resources and index
Identifiers: ISBN 9781098247140 (lib. bdg.) | ISBN 9781098247706 (ebook)
Subjects: LCSH: Baking--Juvenile literature. | Desserts--Juvenile literature. | Baked products--Juvenile literature. | Pastry--Juvenile literature. | Confectionery--Juvenile literature. | Cookery--Juvenile literature.
Classification: DDC 641.8652--dc23

*Scanning QR codes requires a web-enabled smart device with a QR code reader app and a camera.

TABLE OF CONTENTS

CHAPTER 1

THE HISTORY OF DESSERT

Desserts can be traced back to ancient times. The Mesopotamians had a fruitcake-like recipe. The Ancient Egyptians sweetened round, flat breads with dates and honey and cooked them over hot stones.

Much of what we know about the Ancient Egyptians comes from wall paintings in temples and tombs.

The shape celebrated the sun and moon. The Ancient Romans enjoyed simple sweet treats such as fruits, honey cakes, and fruit tarts.

This English oil painting from 1867 shows a first birthday celebration with cake and a candle.

In the 7th century, Persia (now Iran) was one of the first to harvest sugar cane and make cake-like cookies. In the 1500s, sugar became more affordable and widely available. In 1596, a cookbook was published for the growing middle classes in England. In it was a recipe for Fine Cakes. Later, Europeans made it more common to serve dessert, especially cake, for special occasions such as weddings.

Between 800 and 900, the Persians brought sugar cane to Southern Europe.

To this day, desserts help people around the world start the day, complete a meal, and celebrate important **milestones** and holidays. Let's go around the world and learn about pastries from different places and **cultures**!

Almond cake, such as the one in this Ancient Roman mosaic, would have required a great amount of effort to prepare.

Mochi has long been enjoyed in Japan to celebrate the New Year. It was said to harden the teeth and therefore extend life.

CHAPTER 2

PASTRIES FROM EUROPE

Cannoli is a tube-shaped shell of crunchy pastry dough. It is traditionally stuffed with sweet and creamy ricotta cheese, chocolate, and candied fruit. The Italian treat comes from Sicily with different regions showcasing unique ingredients. According to historians, the Cannoli

LEARN MORE HERE!

The crispy Cannoli shell is made with flour, sugar, eggs, and butter.

dates back to between 827 and 1091 when Arabs ruled part of central Sicily. Cannoli are made using sugar cane and almonds, two common Arab ingredients.

Mille-Feuille *translates to "thousand-sheets" in French.*

Mille-Feuille is a classic French treat traditionally made with three layers of puff pastry and two layers of vanilla pastry cream in between. It is then topped with powdered sugar.

Other recipes call for Mille-Feuille to be topped with white and brown icing. Still others finish the dessert with fresh fruit, such as strawberries and raspberries. Any way it is served, it is light, airy, and delicious!

Mille-Feuille should be refrigerated for at least 30 minutes before serving.

BREAD WITH CHOCOLATE

Pain au Chocolat is made from the same dough as a Croissant. However, it is rectangular in shape and baked with one or two pieces of dark chocolate at its center.

The buttery and flaky Croissant is named for its crescent shape. Some historians claim that Marie Antoinette was the first to introduce the crescent-shaped treat to France. It had been a popular pastry in Austria, where she was from. Others argue that the Croissant was brought to France by Austrian baker and businessman August Zang. In any case, the recipe for the Croissant that we enjoy today was created in the early 1900s by French bakers.

Croissant dough is prepared with a technique called lamination. Laminating consists of folding and rolling dough into many thin layers separated by butter. This creates the beautiful layers of flaky goodness!

Marie Antoinette had a sweet tooth, which may be why she is credited with bringing the pastry to France.

The Danish was brought to the Untied States by immigrants.

The Danish pastry came into the world by surprise 350 years ago when a French baker forgot to add the butter during **lamination**. To save the batch of dough, he attempted to fold the butter in. The result was a light and puffy pastry that became loved worldwide. Those from Denmark fill the pastry with cream, fruit, or jam. The Almond Danish is a global favorite. It is stuffed with almond paste and topped with slivered almonds.

Danishes are tasty and filling!

The Kringle is like the Danish pastry, however it was created in Denmark and on purpose. Like the Danish pastry, Kringle is made from buttery, **laminated** dough. The dough is rolled out and shaped into an oval. It is filled with delightful ingredients, such as fruits or nuts, before baking. Once cool, Kringle is drizzled with icing for a little added sweetness.

DID YOU KNOW?

The word "Kringle" comes from the Old Norse word *kringla*, meaning "circle" or "oval."

It is popular to serve Kringle around Christmastime in the United States.

CHAPTER 3

PASTRIES FROM THE AMERICAS

Apple Pie is a **quintessential** American dessert. However, it did not originate in the United States. This sweet and tart treat was brought to the United States by English, Dutch, and Swedish **immigrants** in the 1600s and 1700s. It is often made with puff pastry dough and filled with

EXPLORE LINKS HERE!

After apple pie, pumpkin, cherry, and pecan are the most popular pie flavors in the United States.

apples, butter, sugar, cornstarch, and lemon juice. Cinnamon and nutmeg are popular spices for added taste.

Maple syrup is a less common topping for this silly treat.

Around Christmastime in Quebec, Canada, it is easy to find a sweet pastry with a funny name. *Pets de Sœurs*, French for "Sister's Farts," are French Canadian pastries made from pie crust dough. Before the dough is rolled up, it is covered in a gooey paste of brown sugar, butter, and cinnamon. Once baked, the crunchy dessert (unlike its name) is irresistible!

THE MELTING POT

Most dessert ingredients did not originate in the Americas. European **colonists** brought apple trees and wheat when they immigrated to North America. Sugar was brought by the Spanish and Portuguese.

CHAPTER 4

PASTRIES FROM THE MIDDLE EAST AND AFRICA

Baklava is a sweet and flaky dessert that dates to ancient times in what is now Iraq, Iran, Kuwait, Syria, and Turkey. Because making Baklava is a lot of work, it is often saved for special occasions and religious holidays. Baklava is made using at least ten layers of very thin sheets of dough. Between the layers sit

COMPLETE AN ACTIVITY HERE!

Baklava is a popular dessert throughout much of the world.

finely-chopped nuts, such as pistachios or walnuts. Before baking, the Baklava is cut into pieces. When it is still hot, the baked Baklava is covered in a sweet syrup that melts into each piece.

M'hanncha is flavored with orange blossom and cinnamon, and topped with pistachios.

M'hanncha is a beautiful **coiled** pastry that comes from Morocco. The treat can be made in smaller, bite-size portions. A larger version is often served at small gatherings. To enjoy, guests break off pieces from the outer ring of the dessert. Almond paste is added to the pastry dough before it is coiled.

DID YOU KNOW?

M'hanncha means "snake" in Darija, which is a **dialect** of Arabic spoken in Morocco.

MORE PASTRIES FROM AROUND THE WORLD!

1. Quesitos (Puerto Rico)
2. Sfogliatelle (Italy)
3. Choux (France)
4. Scones (United Kingdom)
5. Kanelbullar (Sweden)
6. Strudel (Austria)
7. Badambura (Azerbaijan)

Countries and **cultures** around the world have their own unique and traditional desserts. Their ingredients and techniques can be similar to or very different from one another.

MAKING CONNECTIONS

TEXT-TO-SELF

Do you like pastries? If so, what is your favorite kind?

TEXT-TO-TEXT

Have you read any other books about food from around the world? What did you learn in those books that was not in this one?

TEXT-TO-WORLD

What are some other ways, besides dessert, that countries and cultures from around the world are special and different from one another?

GLOSSARY

coiled — wound in circles.

colonist — a person who lives in or is a member of a colony.

culture — the language, customs, ideas, and art of a particular group of people.

dialect — a form of a language that is spoken in a specific region or by a specific group of people.

immigrate — to come to live permanently in a country where one was not born. An immigrant is a person who has immigrated.

milestone — an important event or turning point in history or in a person's life.

quintessential — that which most perfectly describes something.

INDEX

DiscoverRoo!
ONLINE RESOURCES

This book is filled with videos, puzzles, games, and more! Scan the QR codes* while you read, or visit the website below to make this book pop.

popbooksonline.com/pastry

*Scanning QR codes requires a web-enabled smart device with a QR code reader app and a camera.